BLAZERS

THE WORLD OF DRAGONS

DRAGON BEHAVIOR

BY MATT DOEDEN

READING CONSULTANT:
BARBARA J. FOX
PROFESSOR EMERITA
NORTH CAROLINA STATE UNIVERSITY

CAPSTONE PRESS
a capstone imprint

Blazers Books are published by Capstone Press,
1710 Roe Crest Drive, North Mankato, Minnesota 56003
www.capstonepub.com

Library of Congress Cataloging-in-Publication Data
Doeden, Matt.
Dragon behavior / by Matt Doeden.
p. cm.—(Blazers. The world of dragons.)
Includes bibliographical references and index.
Summary: "Describes dragon behaviors and habitats"—Provided by publisher.
ISBN 978-1-62065-144-5 (library binding)
ISBN 978-1-4765-1374-4 (ebook PDF)
1. Dragons. I. Title.
GR830.D7D6295 2013
398.24'54—dc23   2012033235

Editorial Credits
Aaron Sautter, editor; Kyle Grenz, designer; Eric Gohl, media researcher;
Jennifer Walker, production specialist

Photo Credits
Capstone: Federico Piatti, 29, Jonathan Mayer, 6–7, 9 (all), 10, 12–13, 18–19, 20–21, 22, 25,
Krista Ward & Tod Smith, cover (top & bottom), Richard Pellegrino, 26; Shutterstock:
Storozhenko, 4–5, Unholy Vault Designs, cover (background), 1, 14–15, Wampa, 16–17

Design Elements
Shutterstock

Printed in the United States of America in Brainerd, Minnesota.
092012   006938BANGS13

TABLE of CONTENTS

ON THE HUNT

As the sun sets, a mighty dragon crawls out of its **lair**. It slowly stands and spreads its huge wings. The dragon is hungry and needs food. With a roar it launches into the sky.

lair—a place where a wild animal lives and sleeps

DRAGON FACT

In some stories, dragons cook their meals with their fiery breath.

The dragon soon spots some sheep. The sheep are easy **prey**. The dragon snaps one up and swallows it whole. Then the dragon grabs a second sheep to take back to its lair.

prey—an animal hunted by another animal for food

DRAGON LIFE

Dragons have appeared in stories and **myths** for thousands of years. The stories are found all around the world. There are many kinds of dragons in these stories. But most share similar **behaviors**.

myth—a story told long ago that many people believed to be true

behavior—the way an animal or person acts

FLYING DRAGONS

- live mainly in mountain caves or old castles
- often breathe fire, ice, or poison
- usually eat deer, sheep, elk, and other large animals

LAND DRAGONS

- live near swamps, ponds, or streams
- have a poisonous bite
- eat rabbits, squirrels, and other small animals

WATER DRAGONS

- live in underwater caves next to the ocean
- have a poisonous bite
- eat fish, squid, seals, and other sea creatures

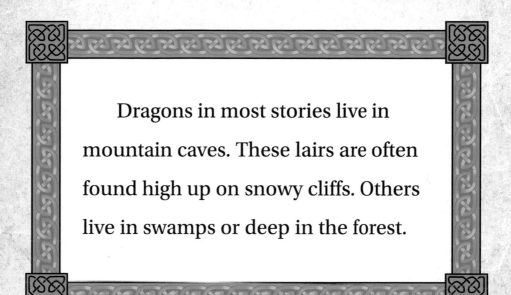

Dragons in most stories live in mountain caves. These lairs are often found high up on snowy cliffs. Others live in swamps or deep in the forest.

DRAGON FACT

Dragons' lairs usually have plenty of hunting ground nearby.

Dragons choose their lairs carefully. They need plenty of space to move around. Dragons also sleep for weeks or months at a time. They like to stay safe in secret underground caves.

Some dragons live in old, crumbling castles.

Dragons in most stories have a treasure **hoard**. Dragons believe treasure gives them power. Some dragons collect gold and gems. Others collect magic rings and swords.

hoard—a large amount of something

DRAGON FACT

Dragons keep their treasure hidden in their lairs.

DRAGON FACT

Powerful adult dragons sometimes eat younger dragons.

16

Most dragons live alone. They usually come together only to **mate**. If a dragon moves into another dragon's area, watch out. Dragons will often fight to protect their **territories**.

mate—to join together to produce young
territory—the land on which an animal hunts for food

Female dragons lay **clutches** of eggs in their lairs. Dragon **hatchlings** are helpless. Their mothers protect them until they can fly and hunt on their own.

clutch—a group or nest of eggs
hatchling—a young animal that has just come out of its egg

DRAGON FACT

In some stories, dragon mothers breathe fire on their eggs to keep them warm.

MIGHTY HUNTERS

Dragons are great hunters. Flying dragons look for food from high in the sky. Others creep through forests to hunt for their meals.

DRAGON FACT

All dragons have excellent eyesight. Flying dragons can spot prey from thousands of feet in the air.

All dragons are **carnivores**. They will hunt far and wide when they are hungry. Most dragons eat land animals like rabbits, deer, and buffalo. Water dragons eat fish, seals, and squid.

DRAGON FACT

In some stories, big dragons even hunt and eat elephants!

carnivore—an animal that eats only meat

DRAGONS AND PEOPLE

Dragons and people are enemies in many stories. Dragons sometimes hunt and eat farm animals like cows, sheep, or pigs. Farmers hate it when dragons steal their animals.

DRAGON FACT

Some dragons have magical powers. They can control people's thoughts and actions with a single look.

DRAGON FACT

Most dragons love riddles. People sometimes escape from a dragon by telling it a good riddle.

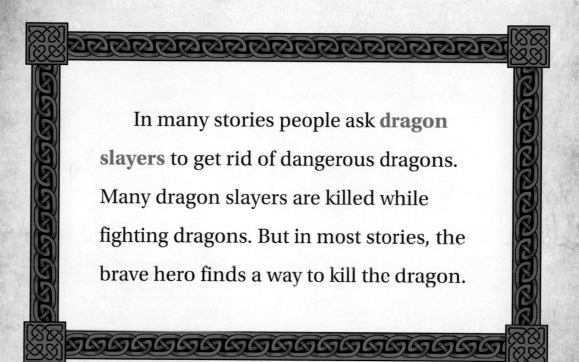

In many stories people ask **dragon slayers** to get rid of dangerous dragons. Many dragon slayers are killed while fighting dragons. But in most stories, the brave hero finds a way to kill the dragon.

dragon slayer—someone who specializes in killing dragons

In some stories from Eastern **cultures**, dragons are friendly. They share their knowledge and like to help people. Whether they are fierce or friendly, dragons are amazing mythical creatures.

DRAGON FACT

In rare cases, a dragon might share a close friendship with someone. These dragons may even allow their human friends to ride on them.

culture—a people's way of life, ideas, customs, and traditions

GLOSSARY

behavior (bee-HAY-vyuhr)—the way an animal or person acts

carnivore (KAHR-nuh-vohr)—an animal that eats only meat

clutch (KLUHCH)—a group or nest of eggs

culture (KUHL-chur)—a people's way of life, ideas, customs, and traditions

dragon slayer (DRAG-uhn SLAY-uhr)—someone who specializes in killing dragons

hatchling (HACH-ling)—a young animal that has just come out of its egg

hoard (HORD)—a large amount of something

lair (LAIR)—a place where a wild animal lives and sleeps

mate (MATE)—to join together to produce young

myth (MITH)—a story told long ago that many people believed to be true

prey (PRAY)—an animal hunted by another animal for food

territory (TER-uh-tor-ee)—the land on which an animal hunts for food and raises its young

READ MORE

Morris, Susan J. *A Practical Guide to Dragon Magic.* Renton, Wash.: Wizards of the Coast, 2010.

Steer, Dugald A., ed. *Dragonology: Bringing Up Baby Dragons.* Somerville, Mass.: Candlewick Press, 2008.

Troupe, Thomas Kingsley. *The Truth about Dragons.* Fairy-tale Superstars. Mankato, Minn.: Picture Window Books, 2010.

INTERNET SITES

FactHound offers a safe, fun way to find Internet sites related to this book. All of the sites on FactHound have been researched by our staff.

Here's all you do:

Visit *www.facthound.com*

Type in this code: 9781620651445

Super-cool stuff! Check out projects, games and lots more at **www.capstonekids.com**

INDEX